Easy Piano Music Sheet for Kids

**From Beginner to Pianist
Quickly and Easily Listen,
Read and Learn
47 Famous Songs
in Order of Difficulty
(Free Audio)**

How to listen to audio:

It is possible to listen or download all the mp3 audio tracks by accessing the following link:

https://urly.it/3n-gw

or by scanning the QR Code:

Layout: Mauro Costa

INDEX

Merrily we Roll Along

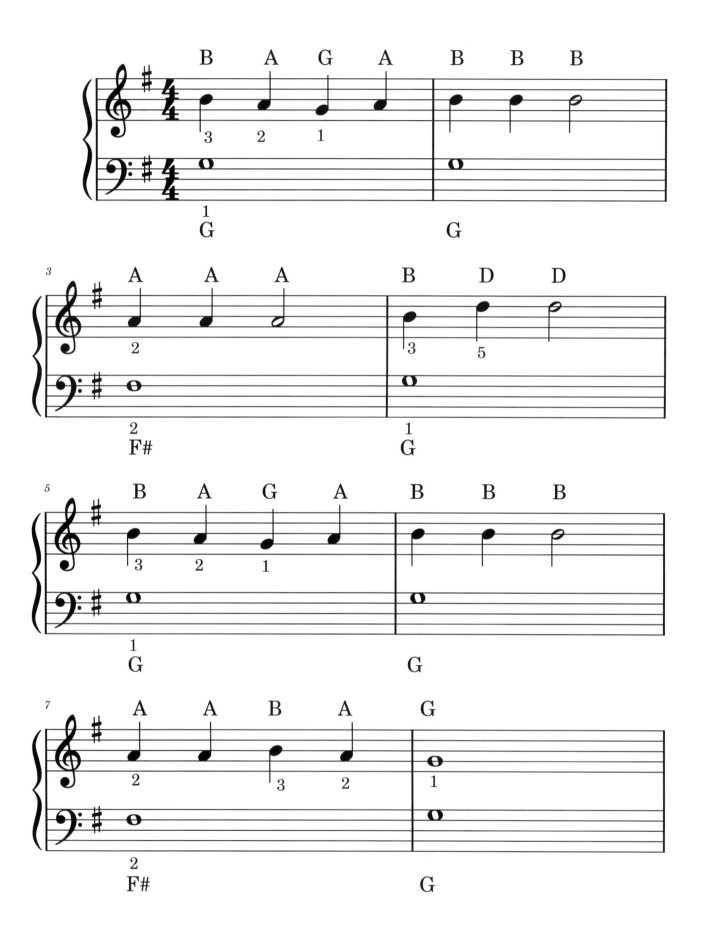

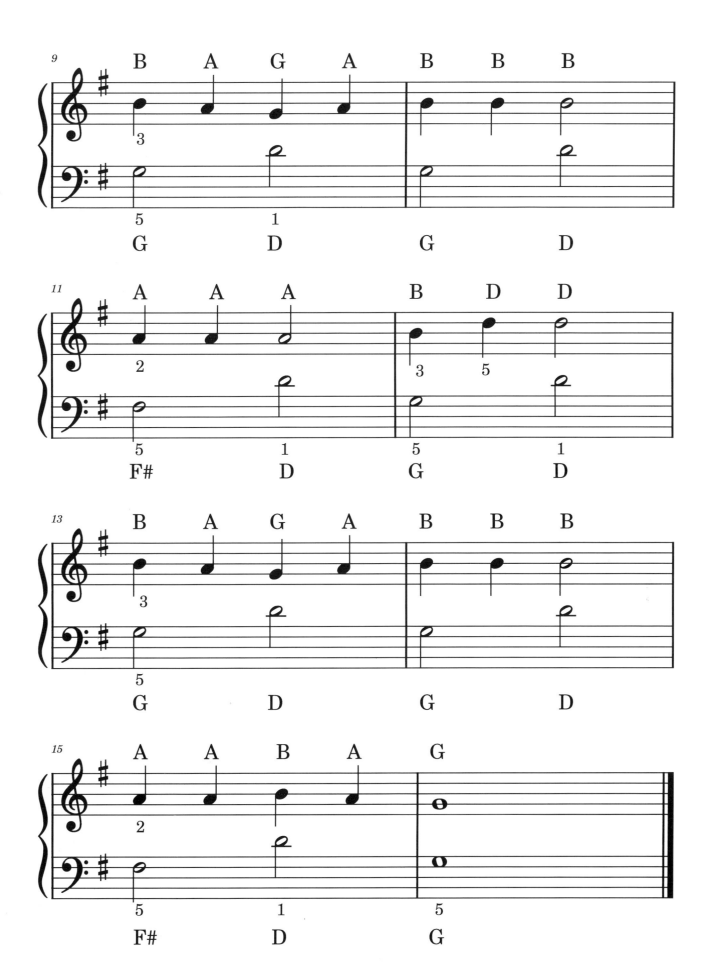

Ring a Ring of Roses

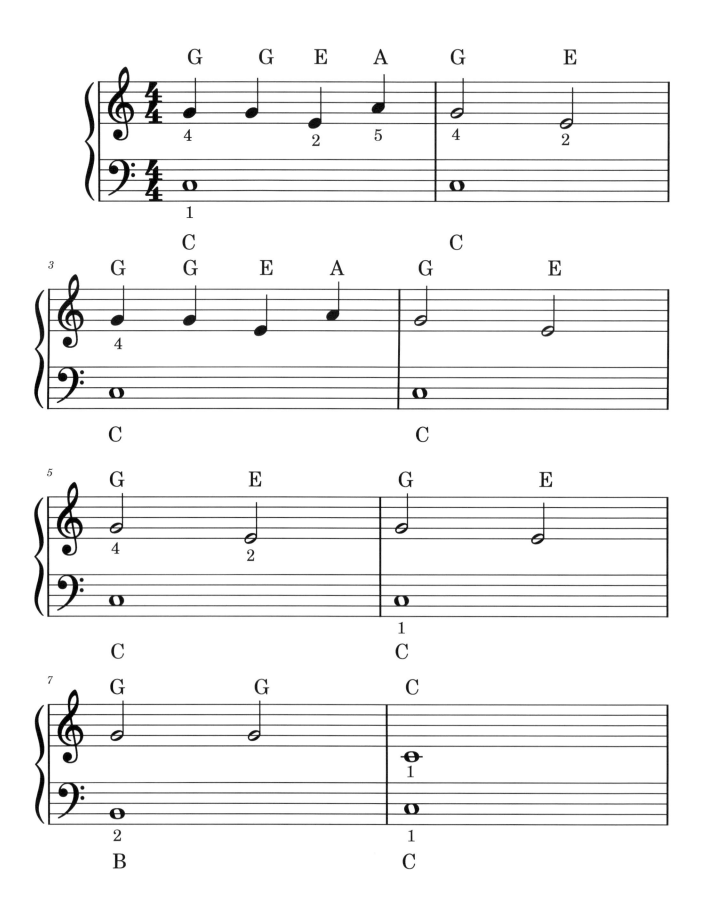

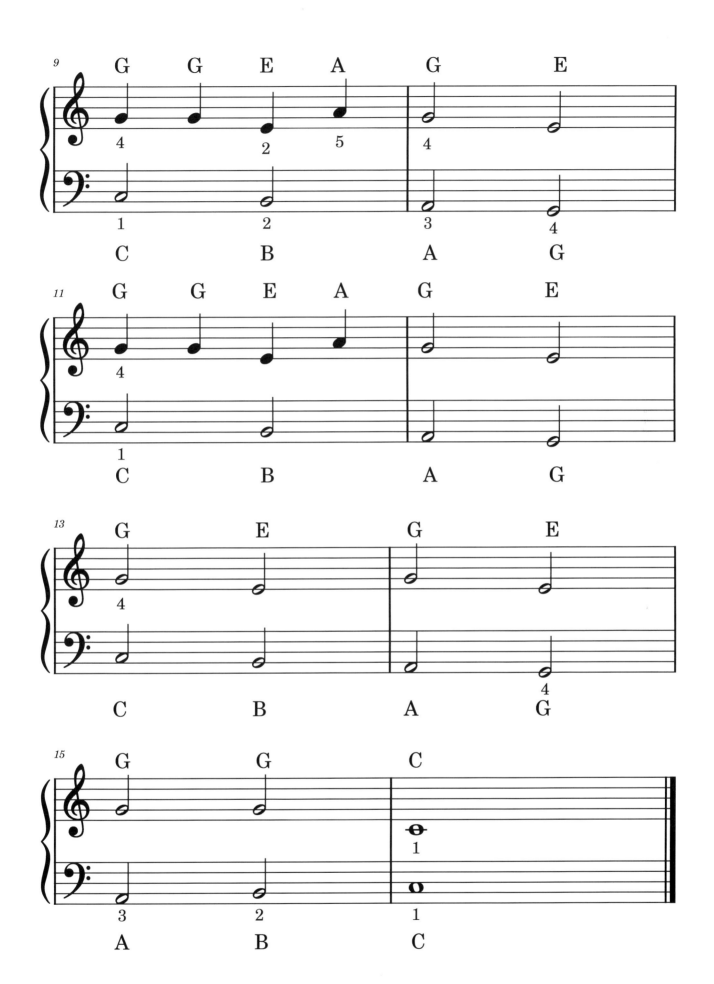

Ode to Joe

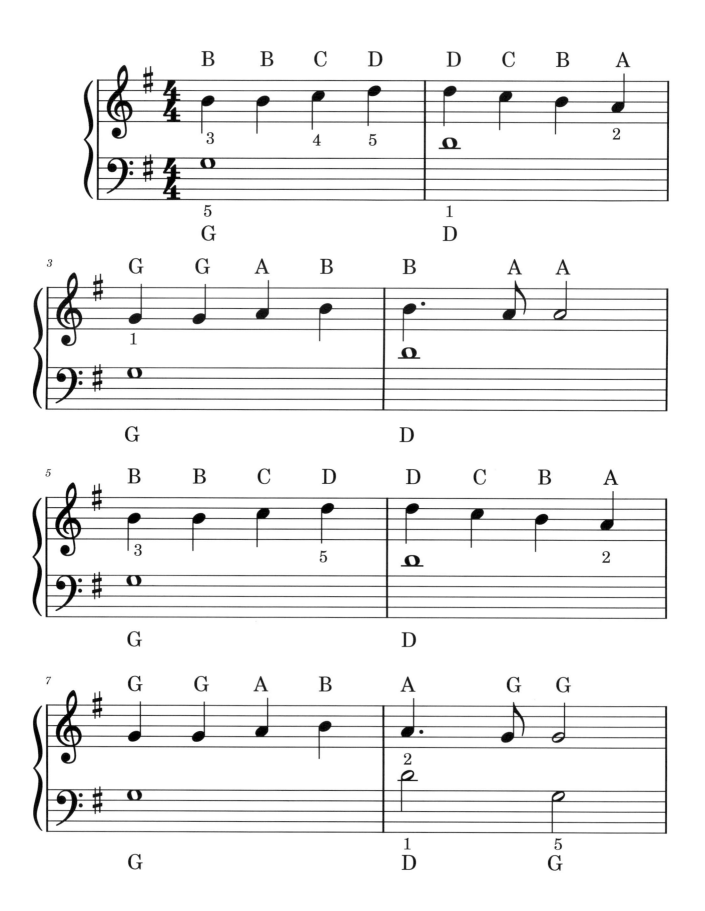

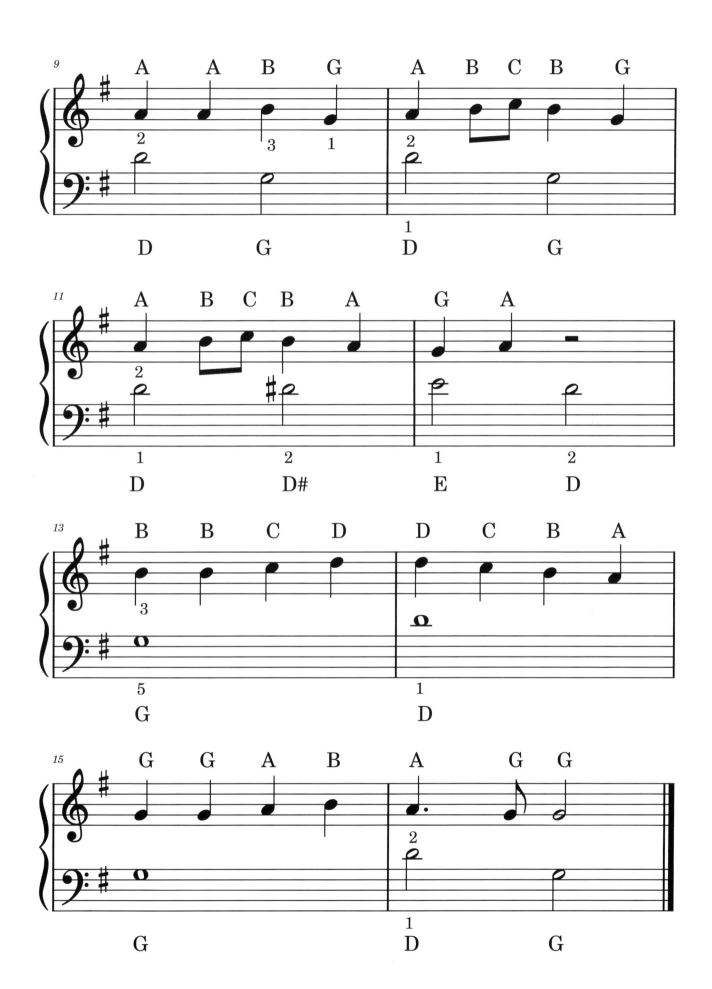

Rain, Rain, Go Away

Hot Cross Buns

London Bridge

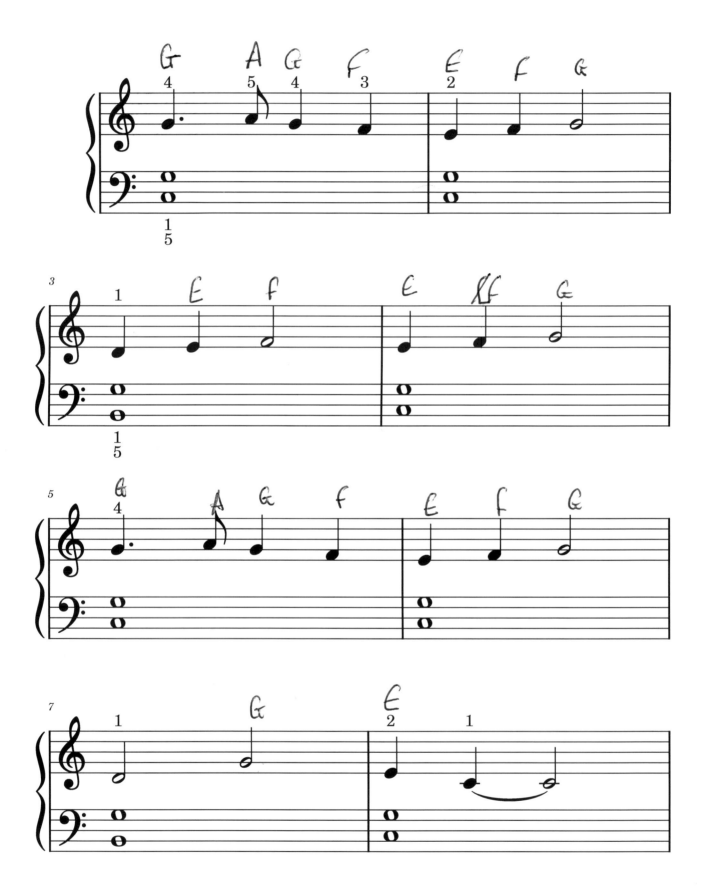

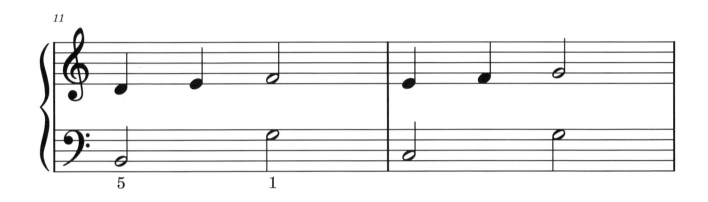

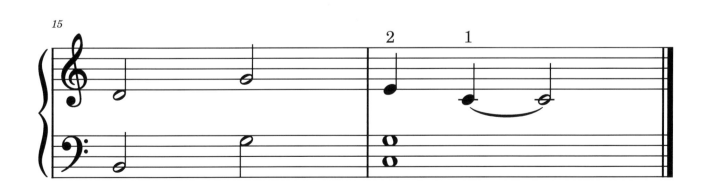

15

This Old Man

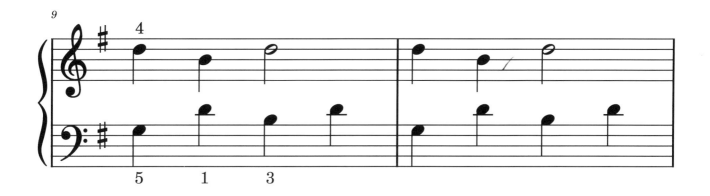

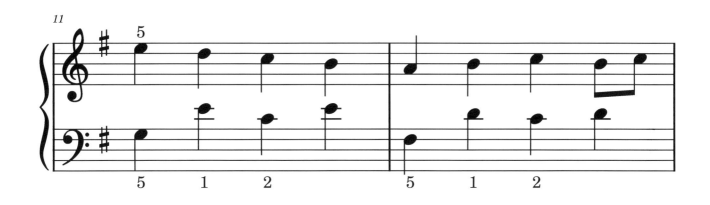

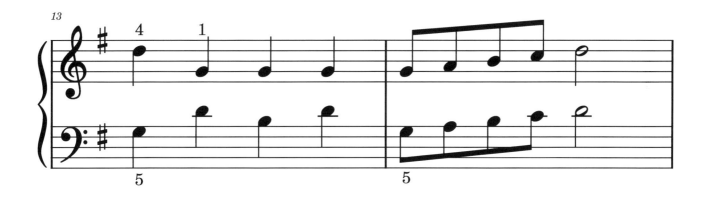

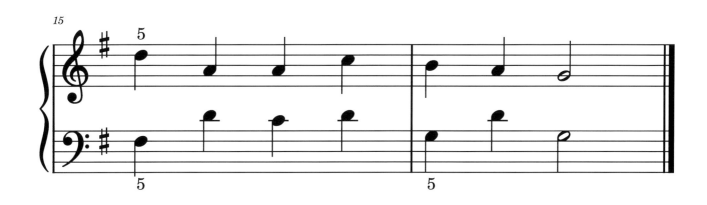

Alouette

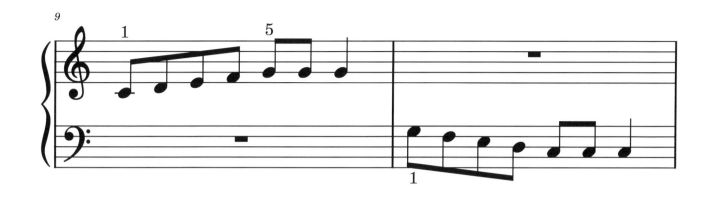

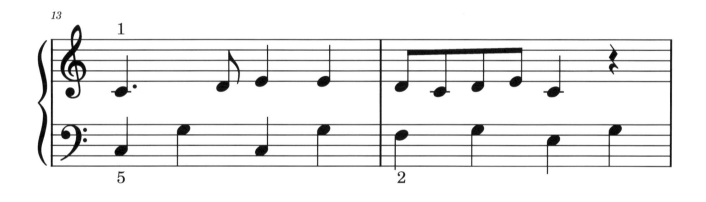

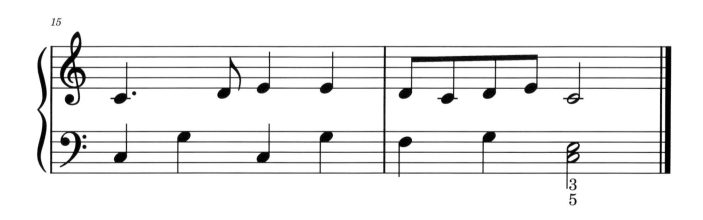

Old MacDonald Had a Farm

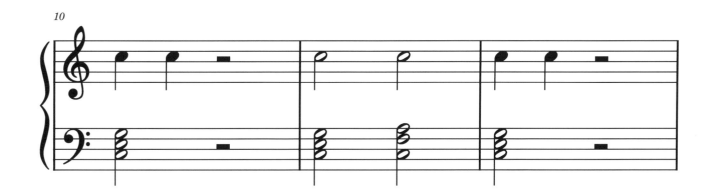

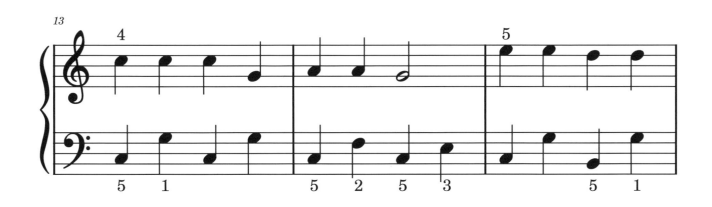

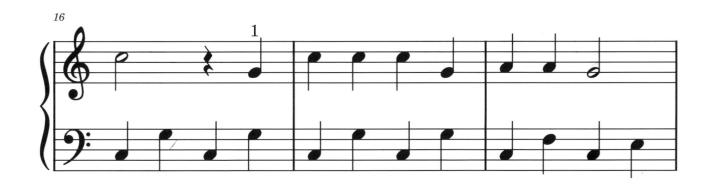

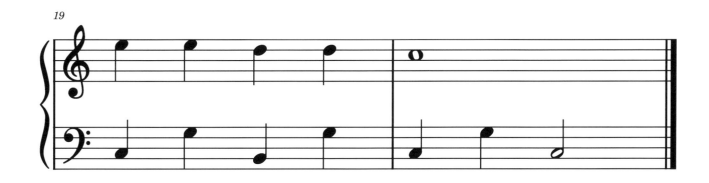

Lightly Row

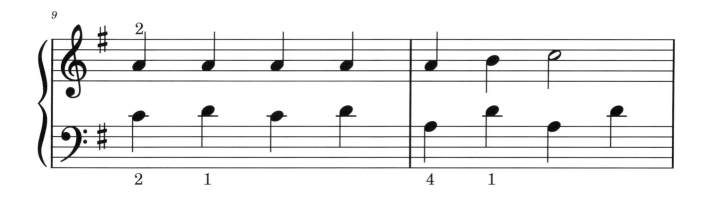

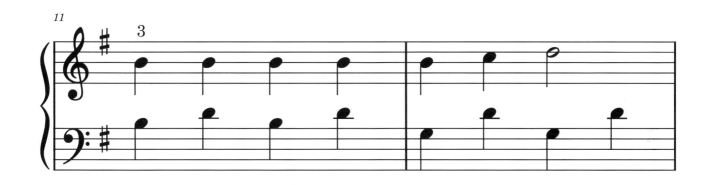

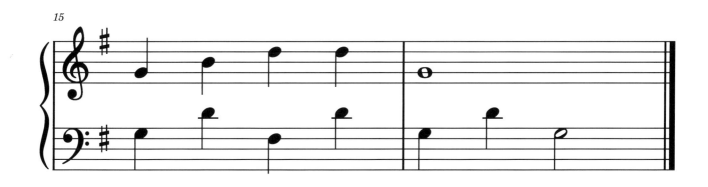

Skip to My Lou

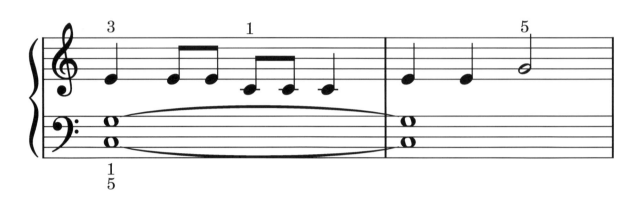

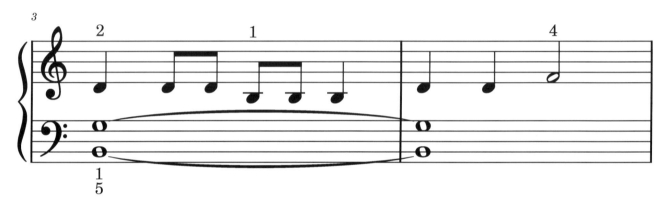

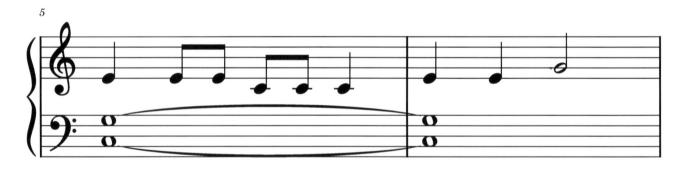

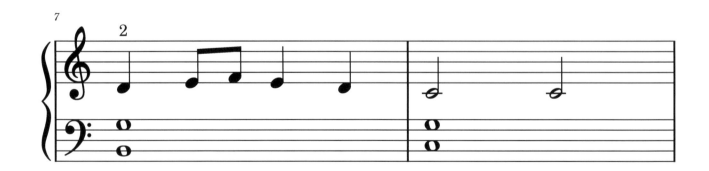

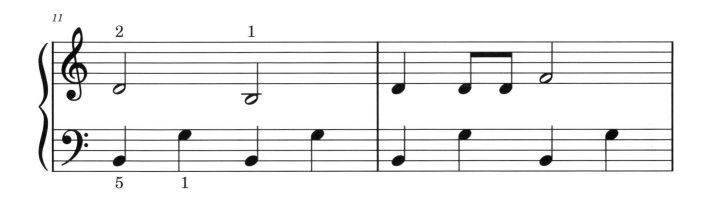

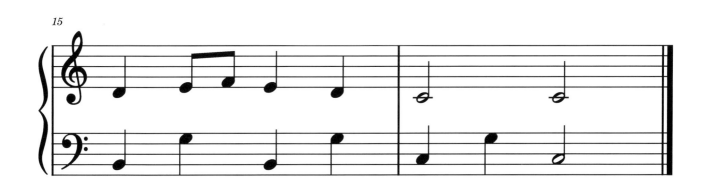

The Muffin Man

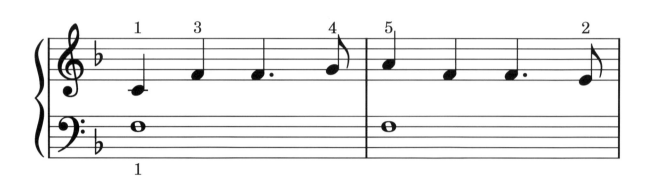

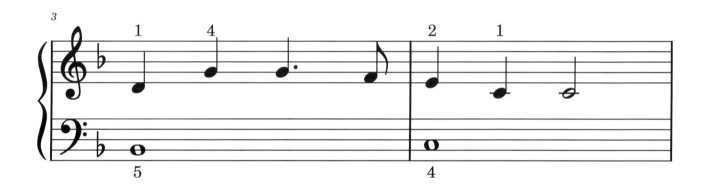

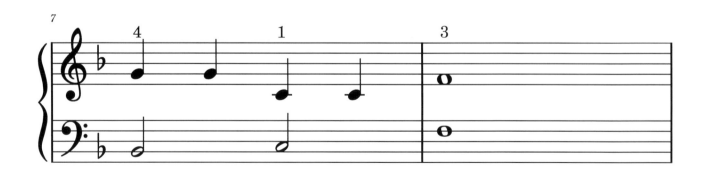

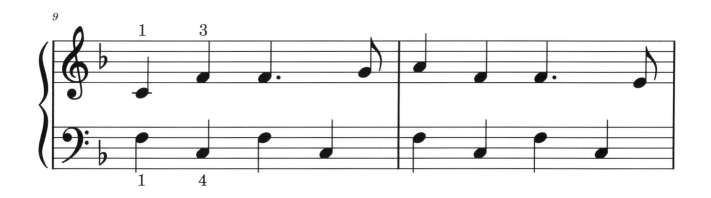

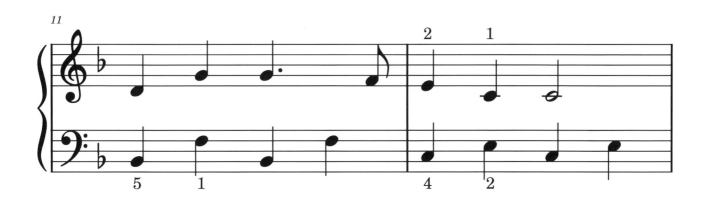

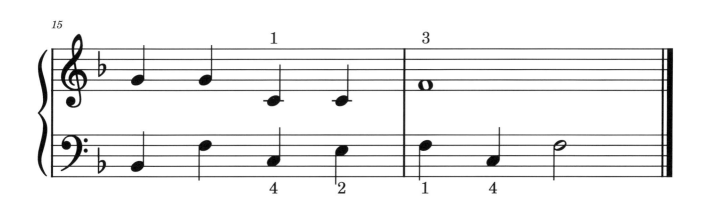

Hickory, Dickory, Dock

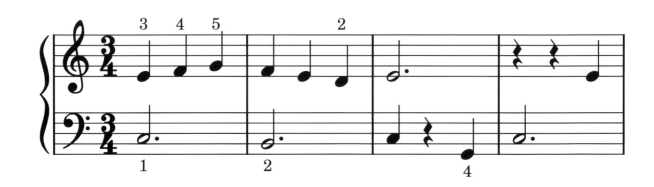

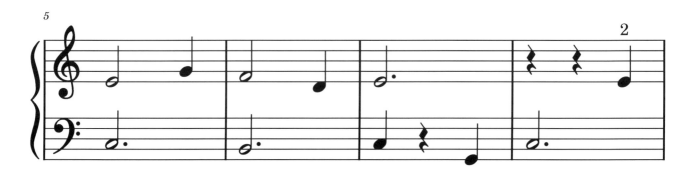

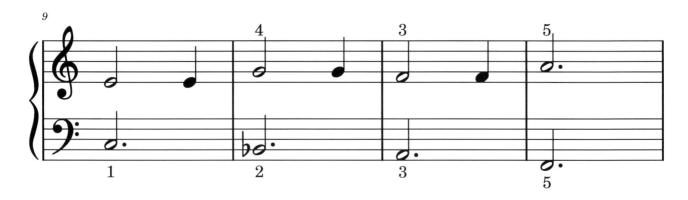

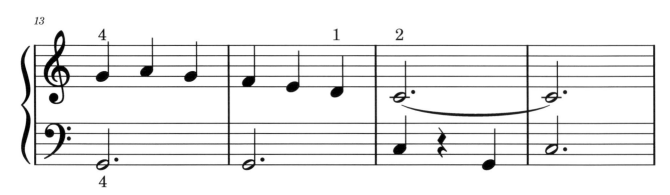

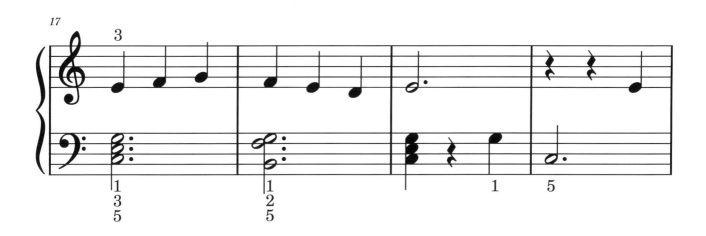

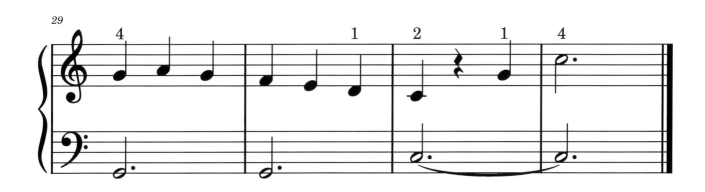

Hush, Little Baby

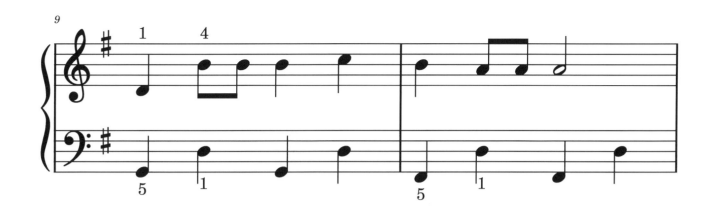

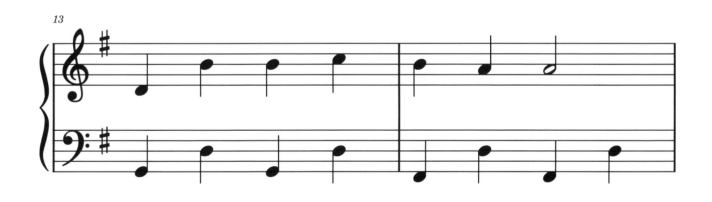

Pop Goes the Weasel

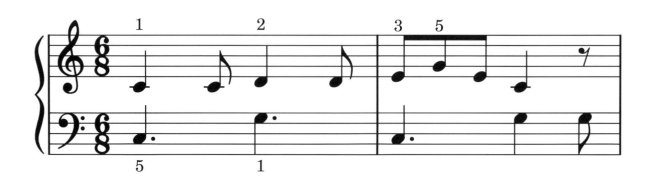

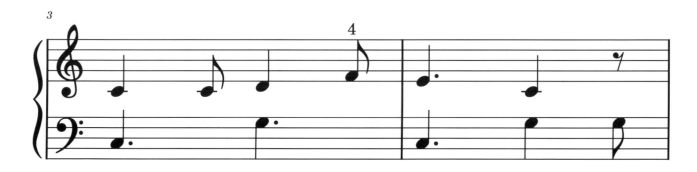

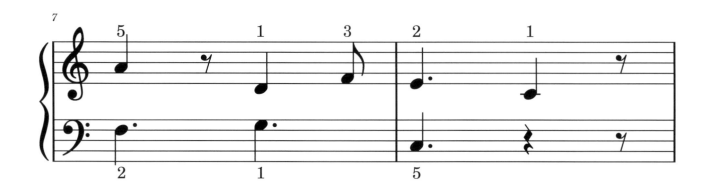

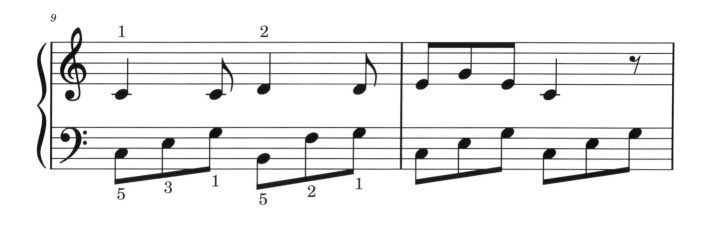

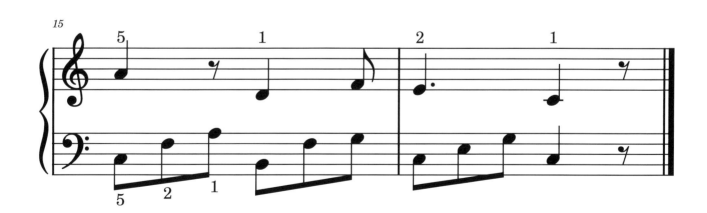

Scotland the Brave

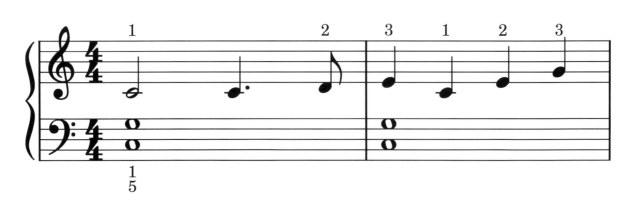

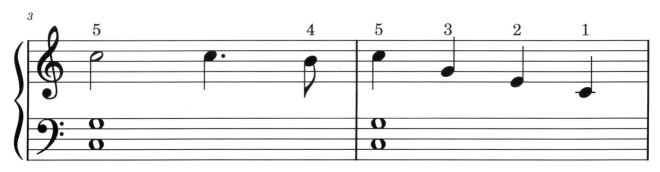

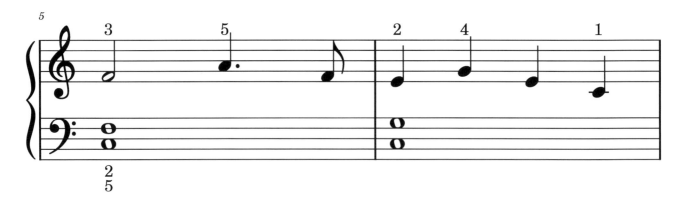

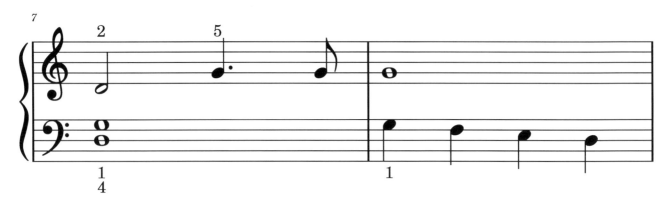

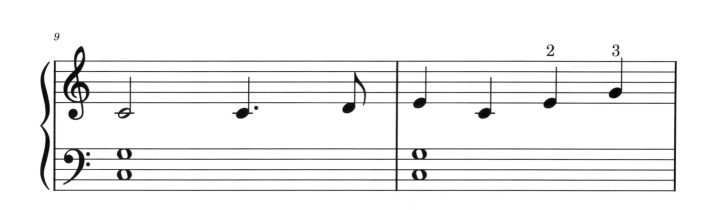

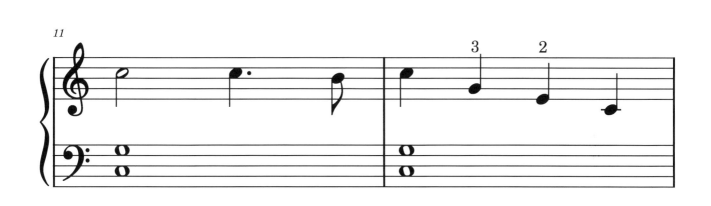

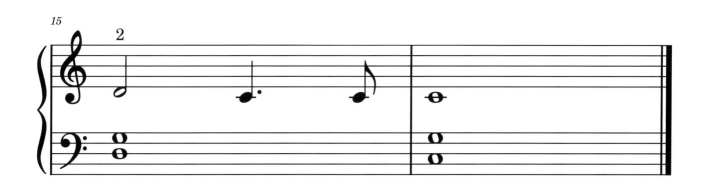

35

Row, Row, Row Your Boat

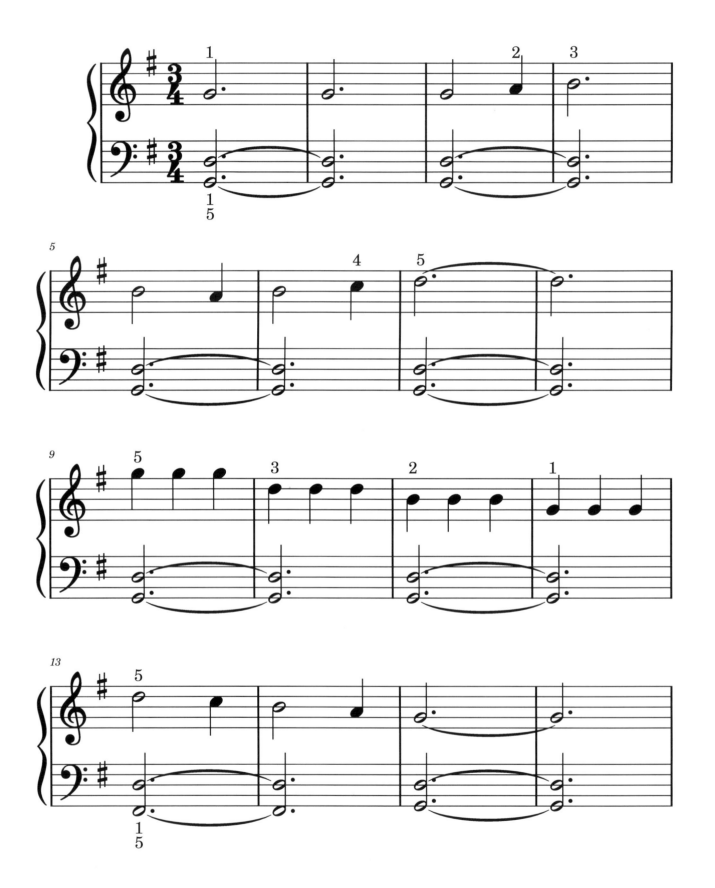

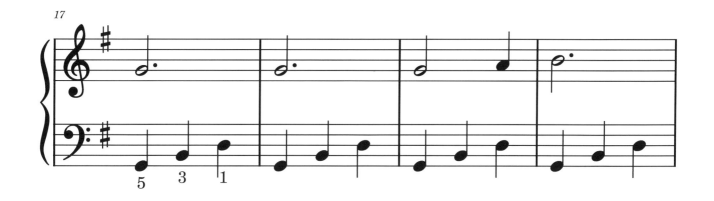

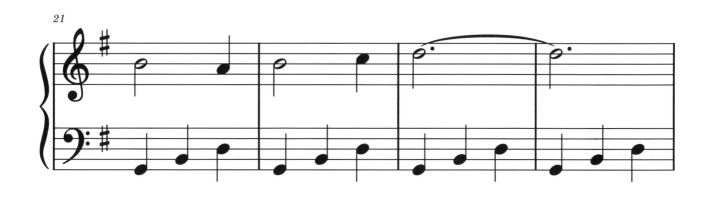

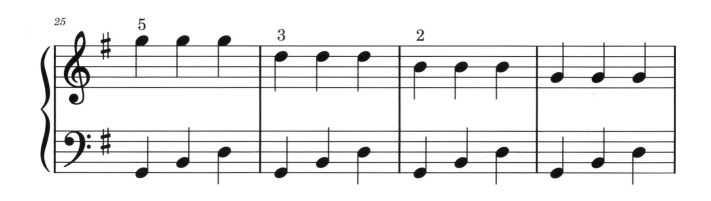

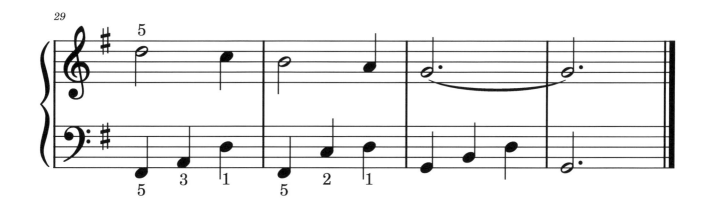

Happy Birthday

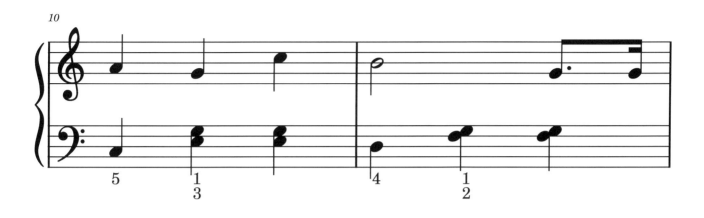

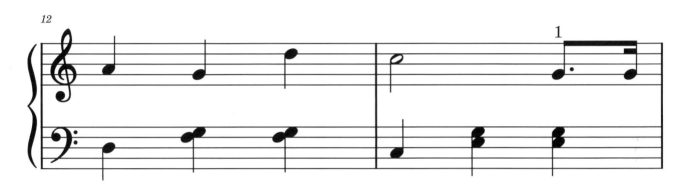

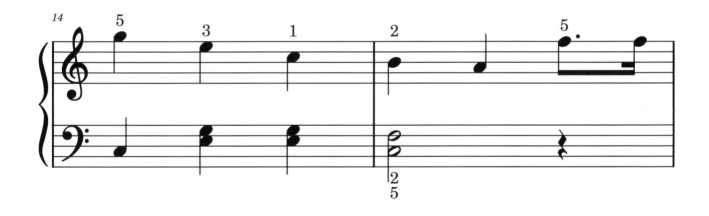

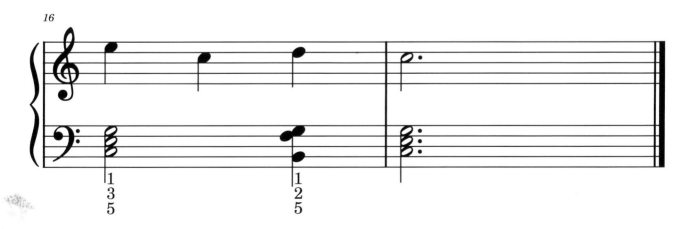

When the Saints Go Marching In

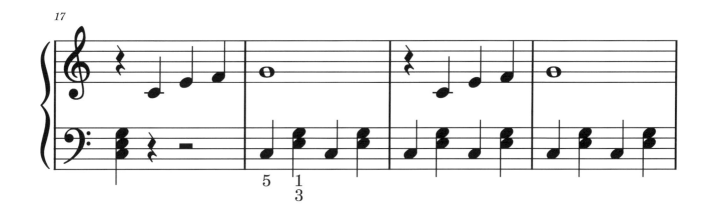

Sur le Pont d'Avignon

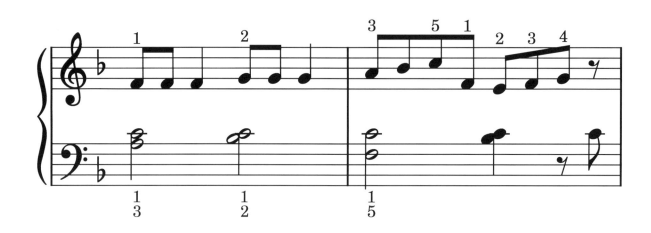

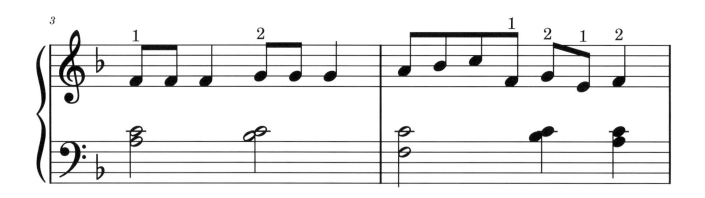

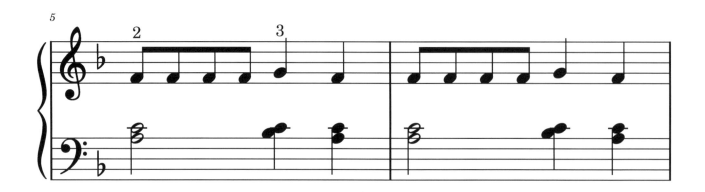

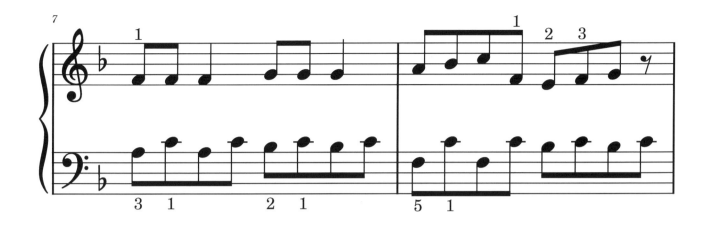

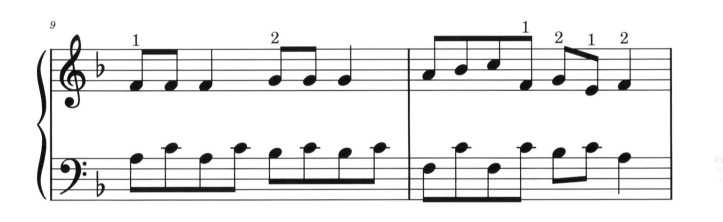

Oh Susanna

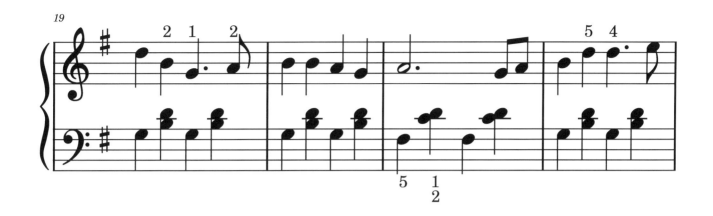

45

Twinkle, Twinkle, Little Star

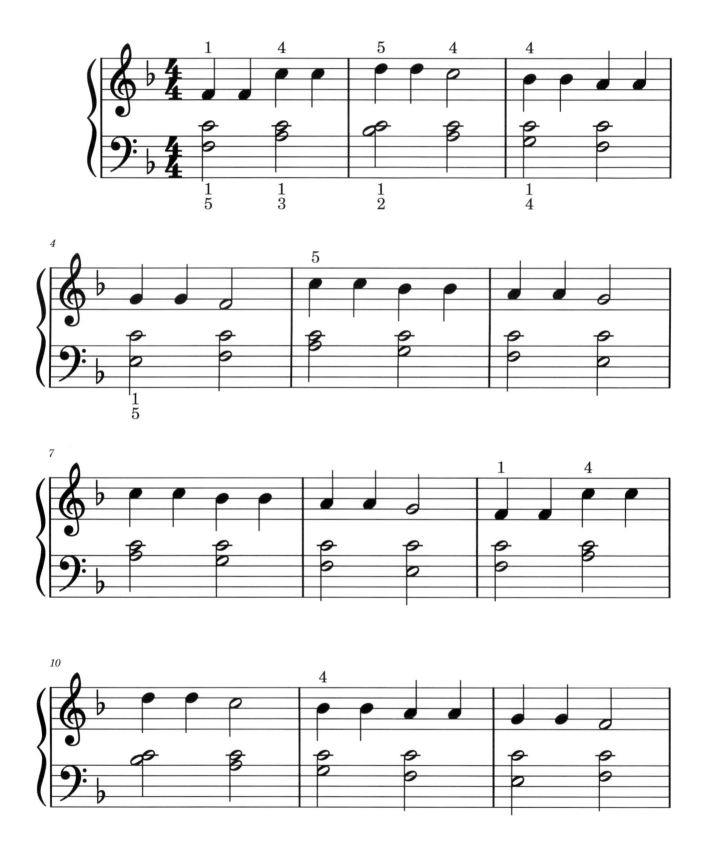

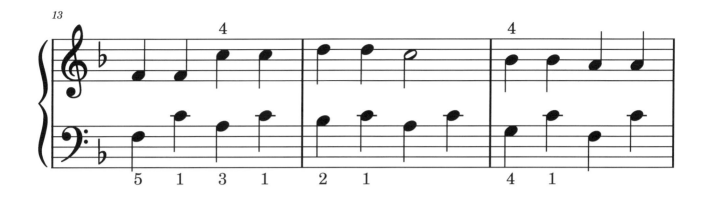

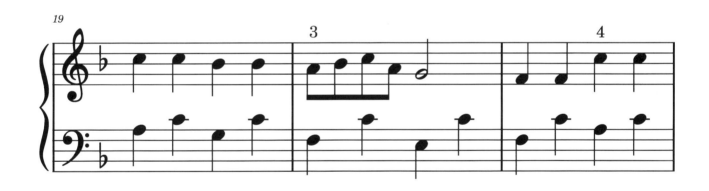

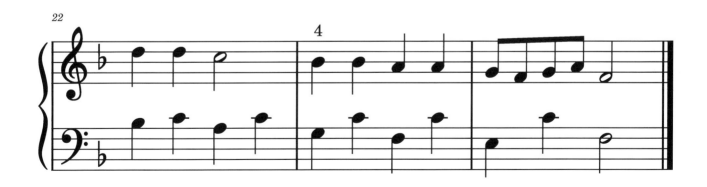

Are You Sleeping- Frère Jacques

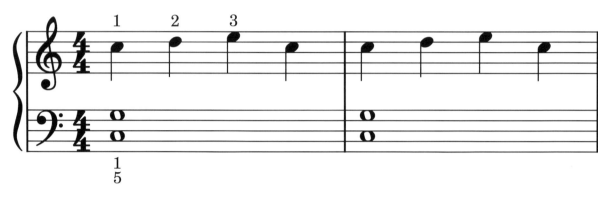

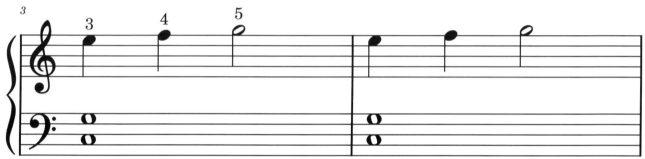

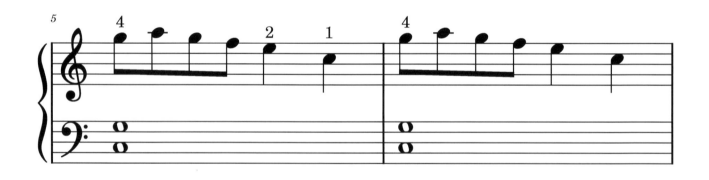

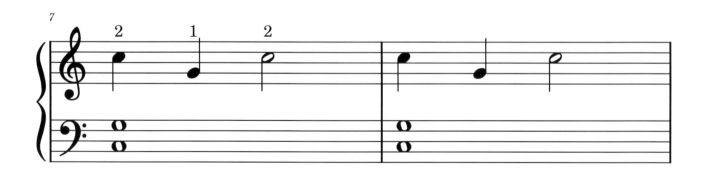

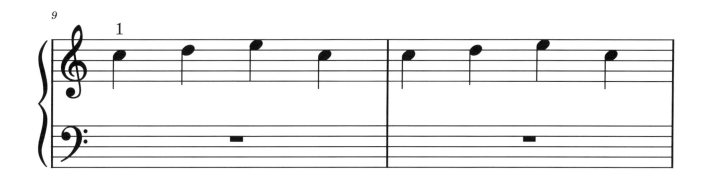

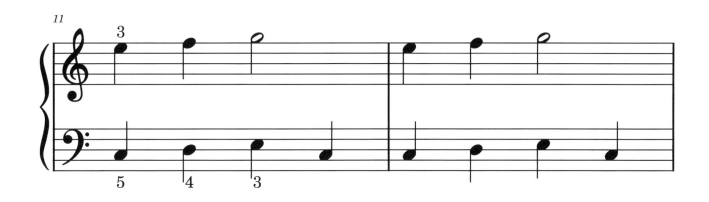

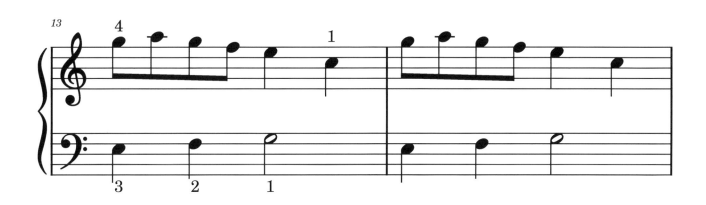

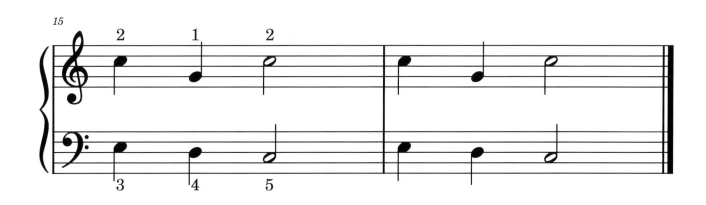

The Wheels on the Bus

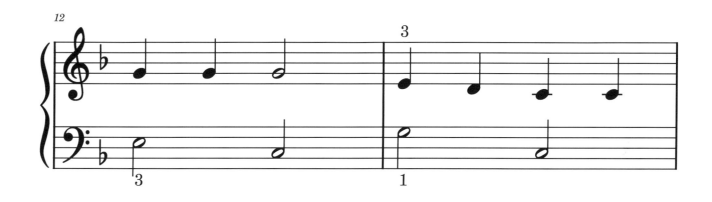

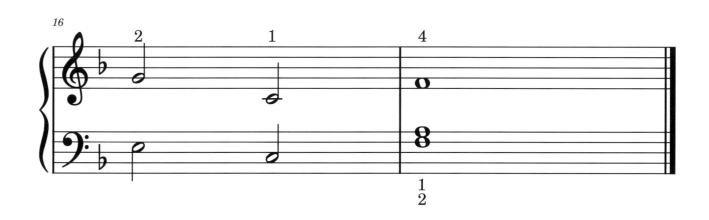

Itsy Bitsy Spider

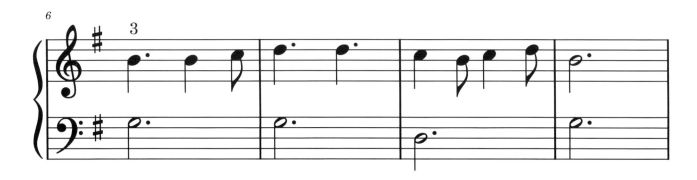

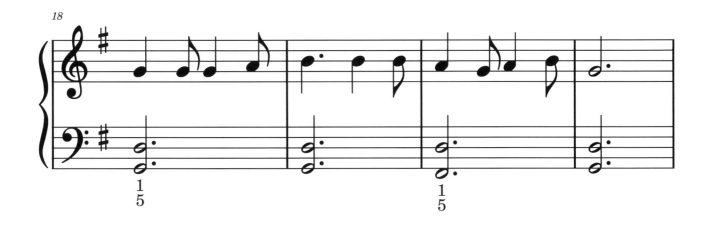

Yankee Doodle

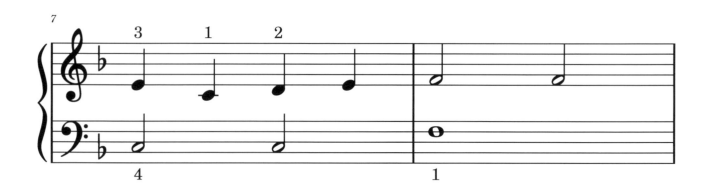

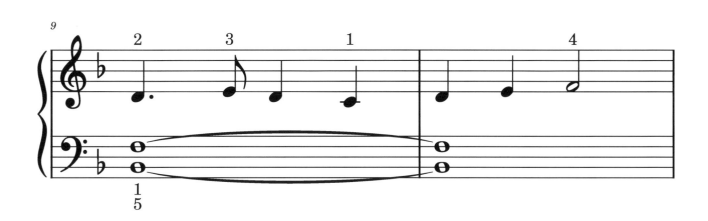

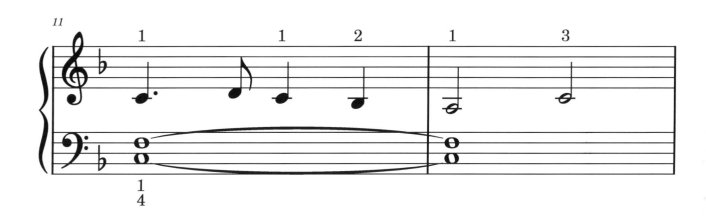

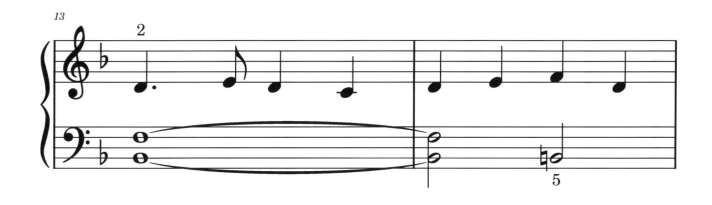

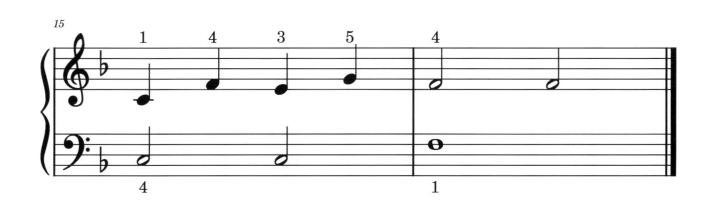

Humpty Dumpty

Head, Shoulders, Knees and Toes

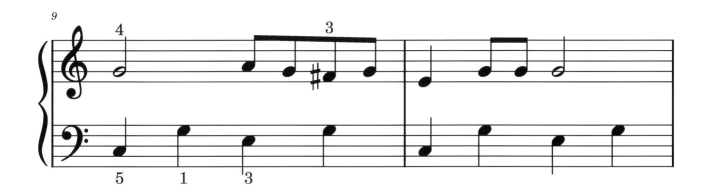

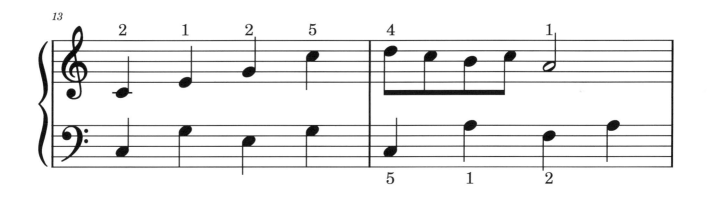

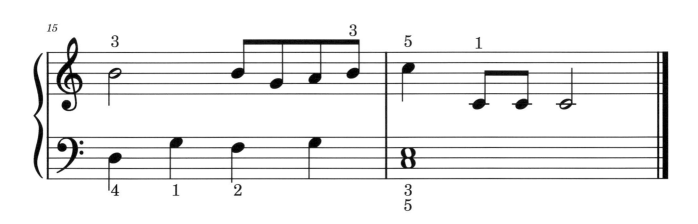

She'll Be Coming Round the Mountain

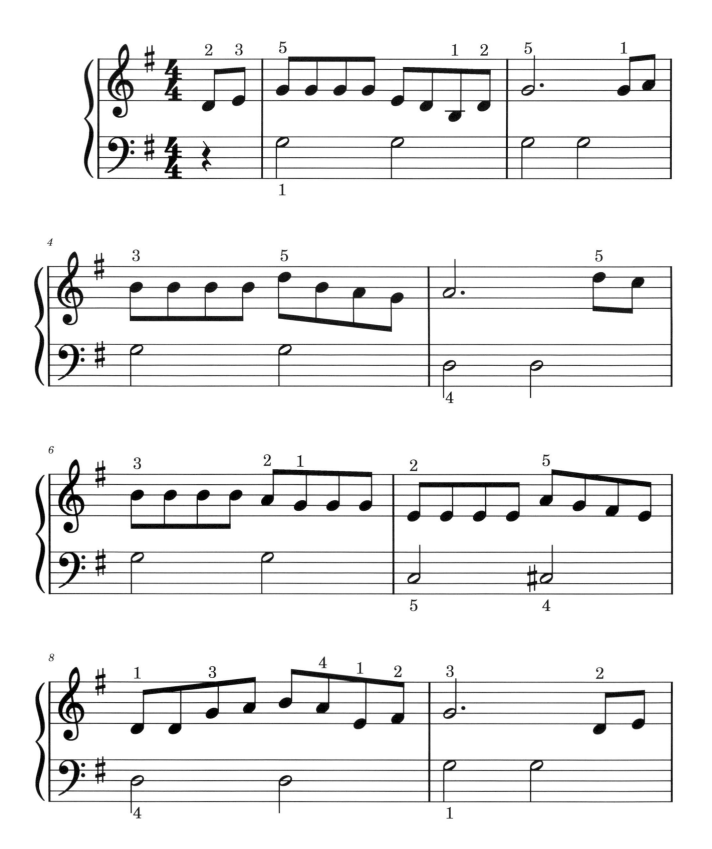

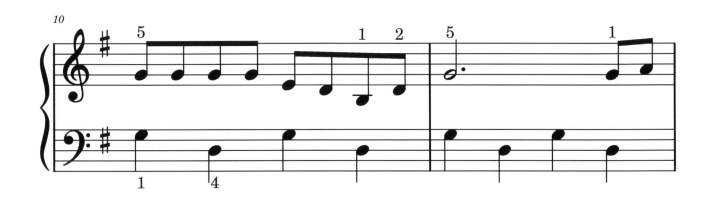

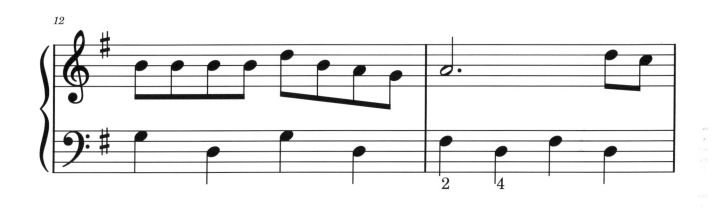

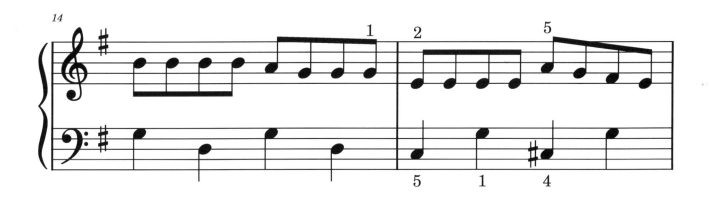

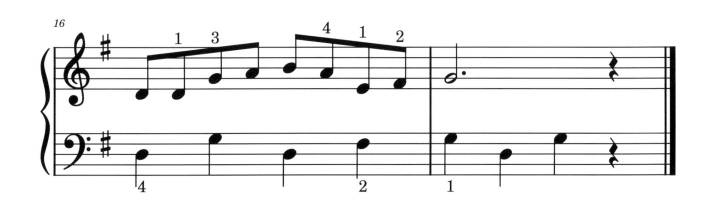

Three Blind Mice

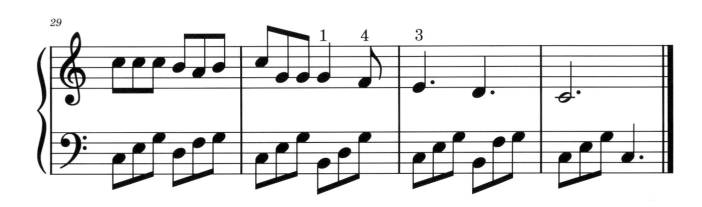

Rock-A-Bye Baby

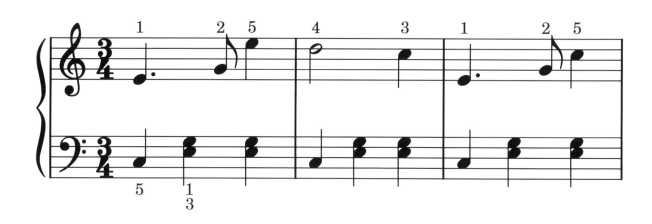

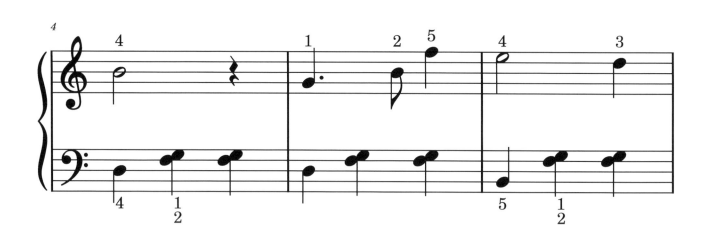

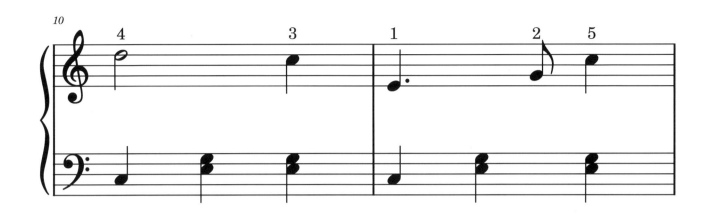

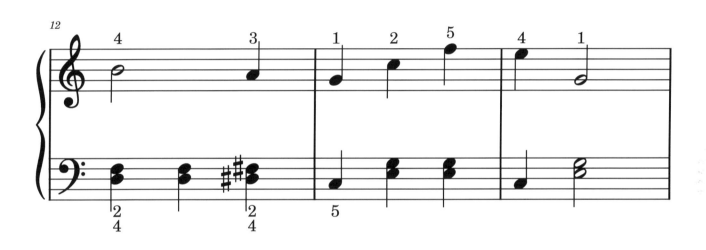

Bingo

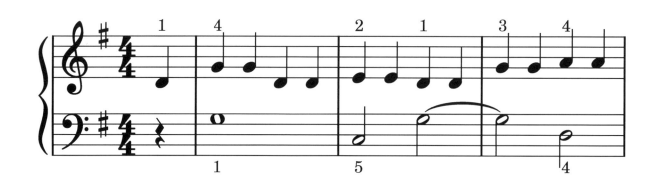

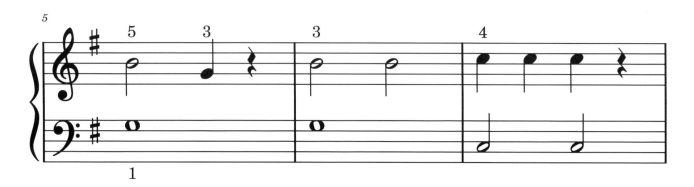

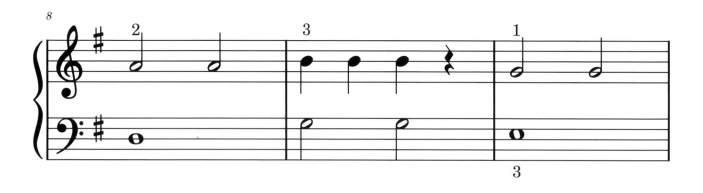

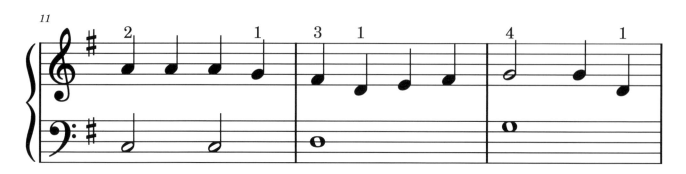

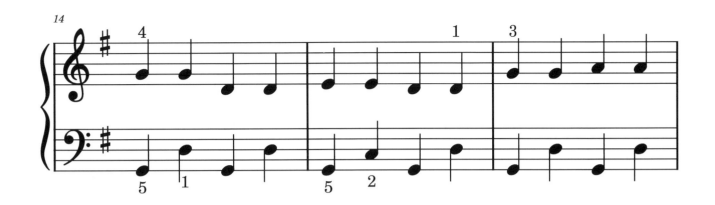

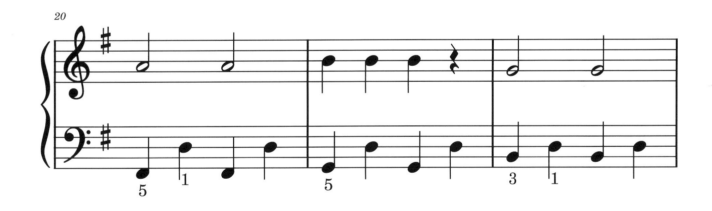

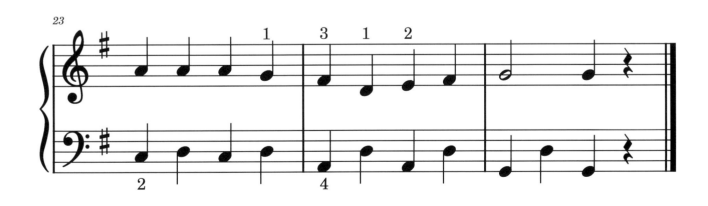

Sing a Song of Sixpence

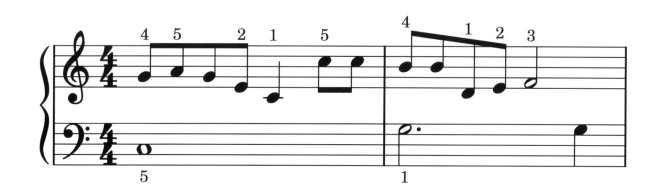

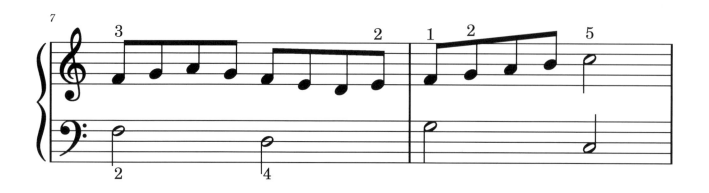

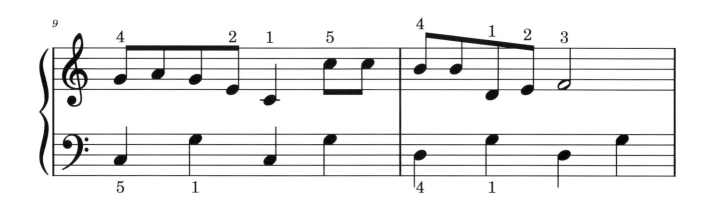

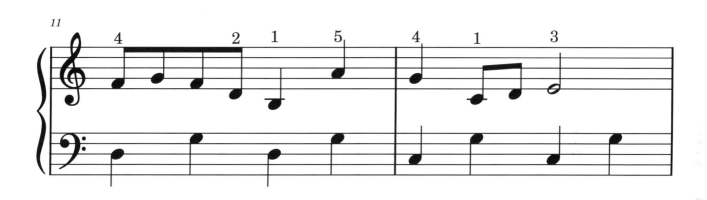

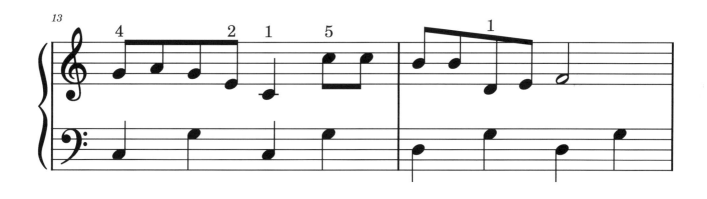

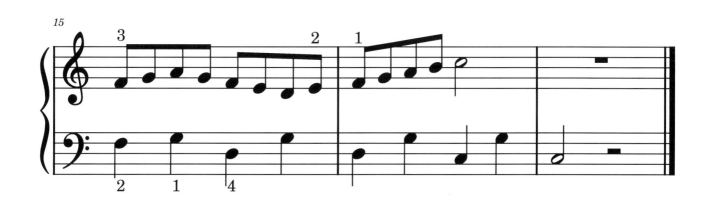

For He's a Jolly Good Fellow

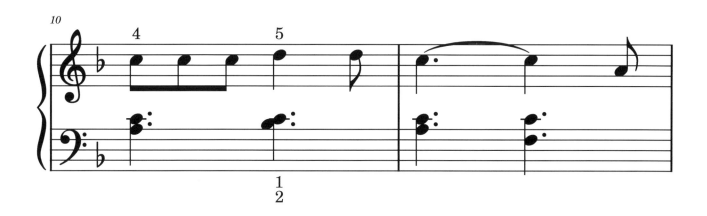

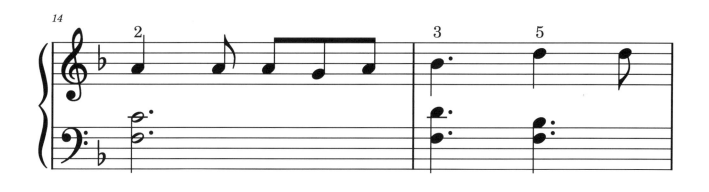

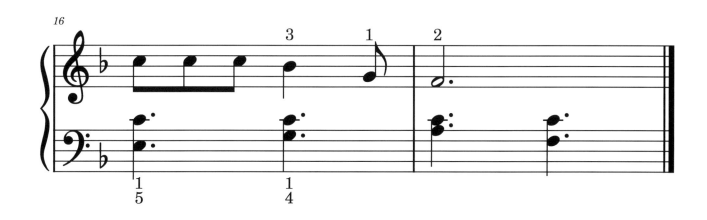

Take Me Out To the Ballgame

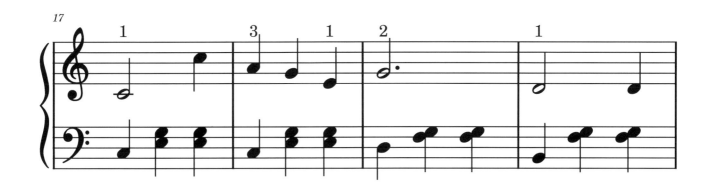

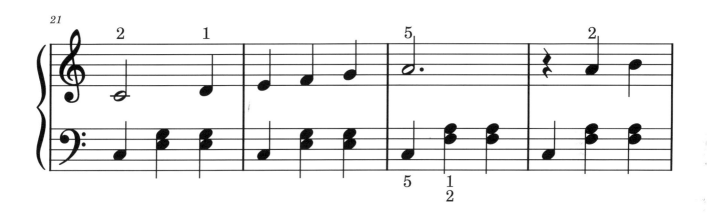

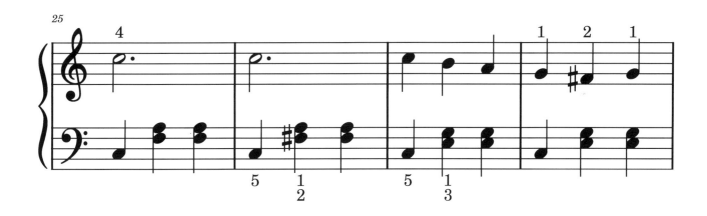

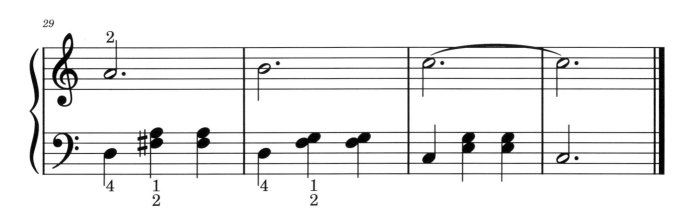

Hey Diddle Diddle

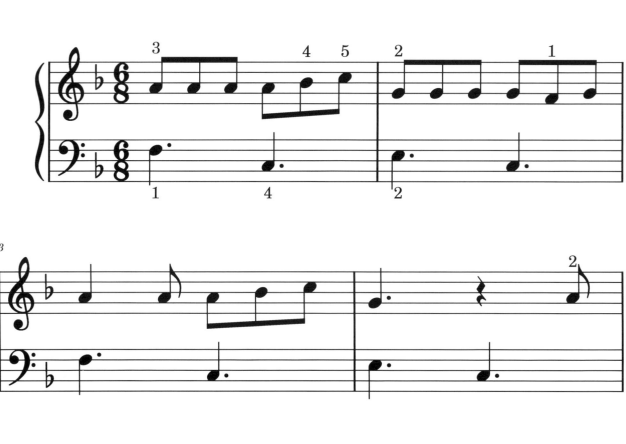

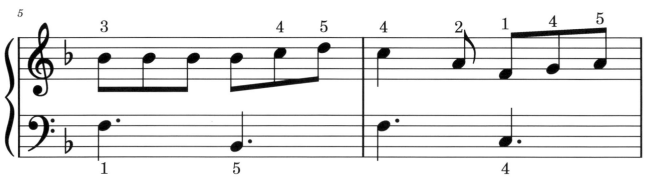

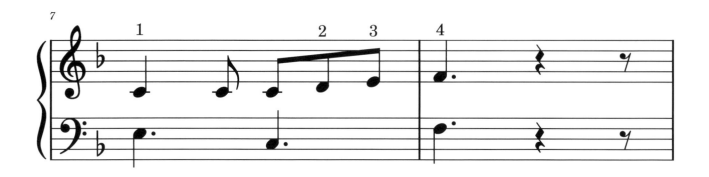

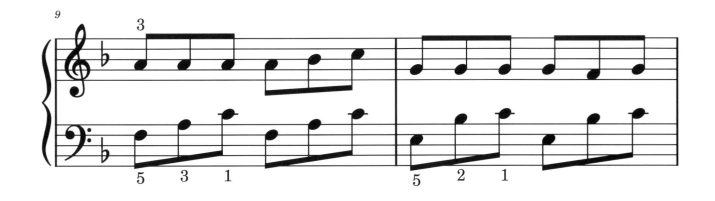

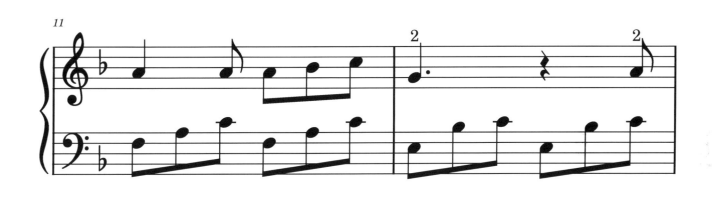

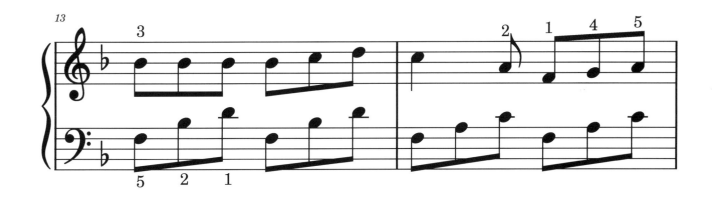

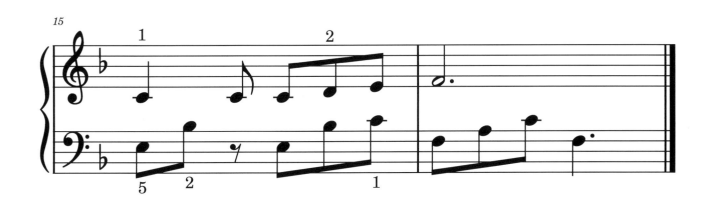

Polly Put the Kettle On

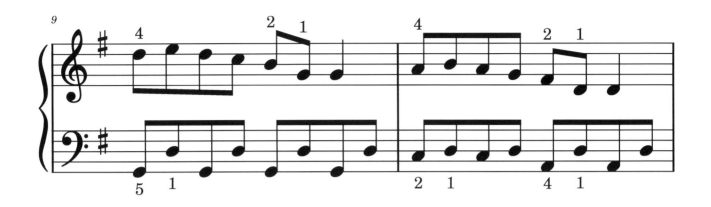

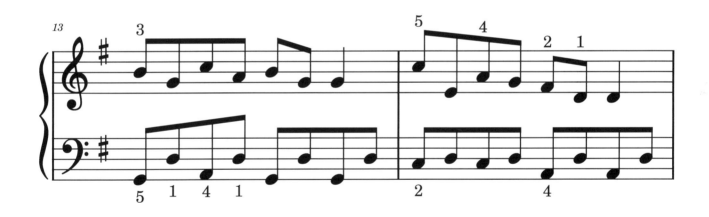

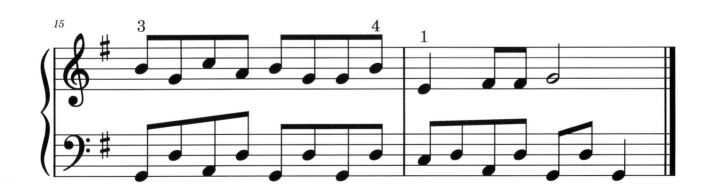

Für Elise

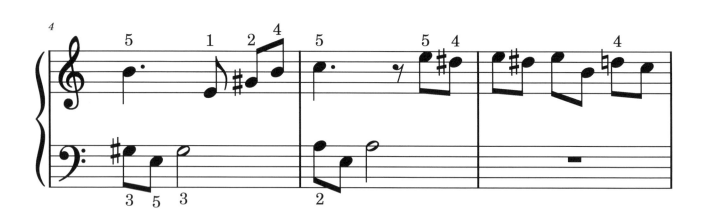

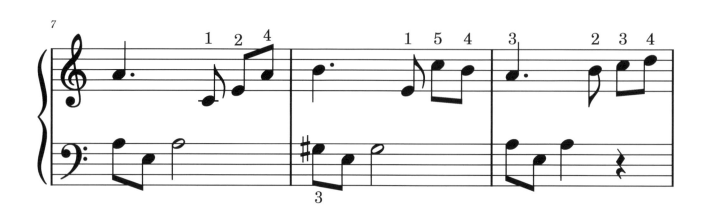

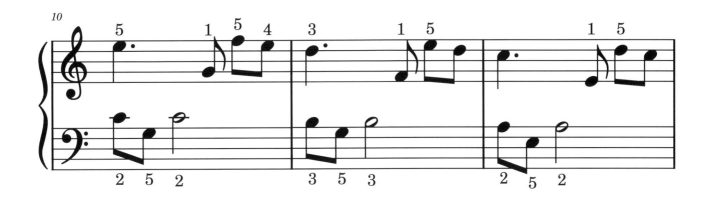

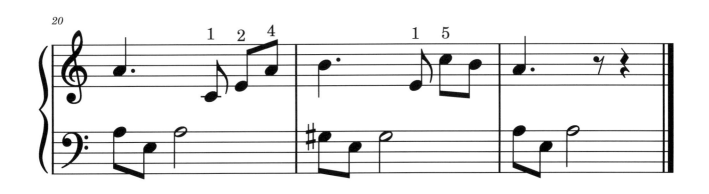

Oh My Darling Clementine

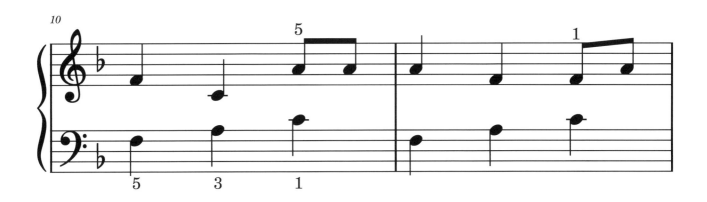

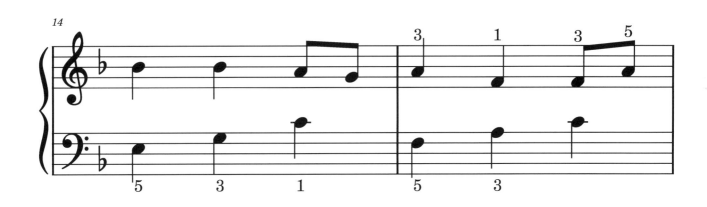

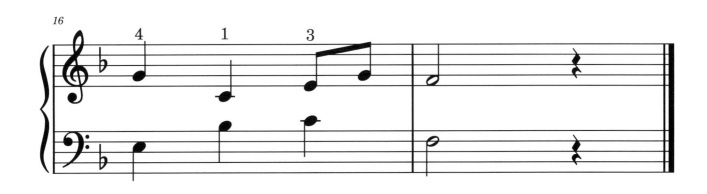

America, The Beautiful

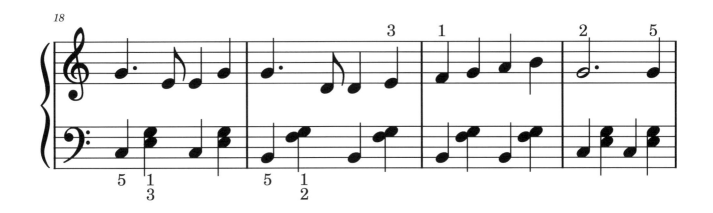

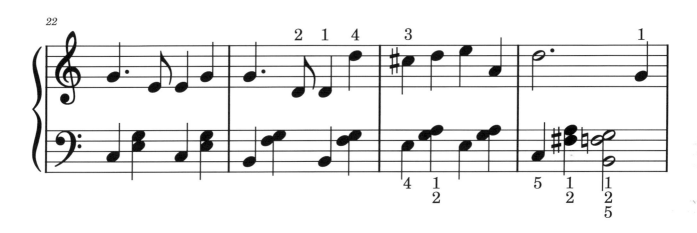

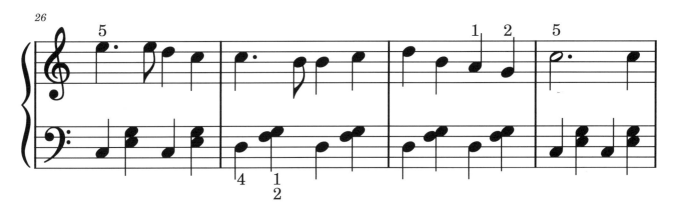

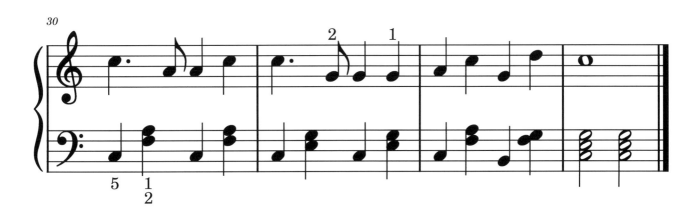

Tarantella Napoletana

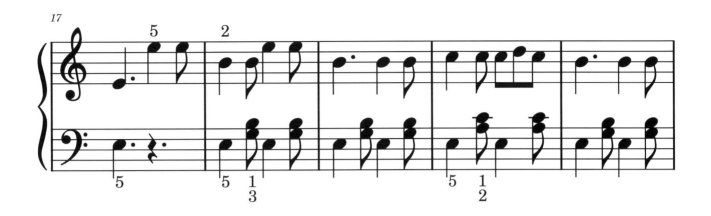

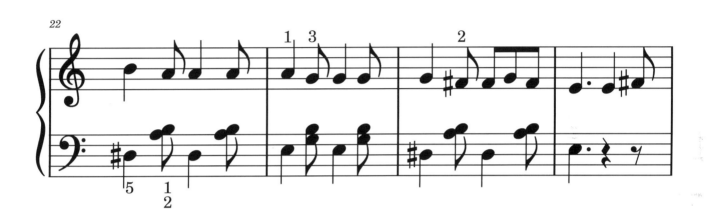

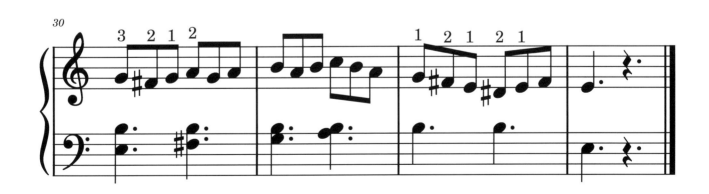

Bella Ciao

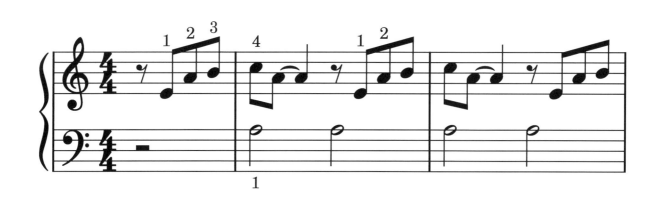

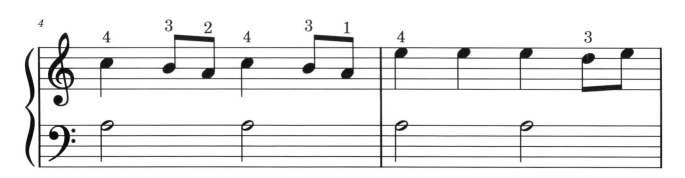

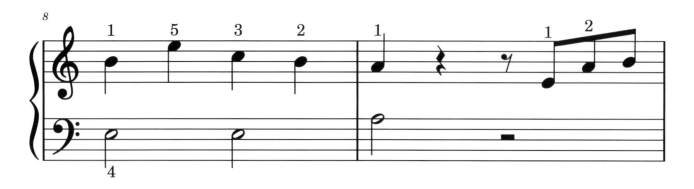

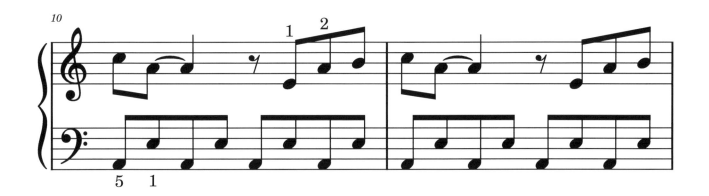

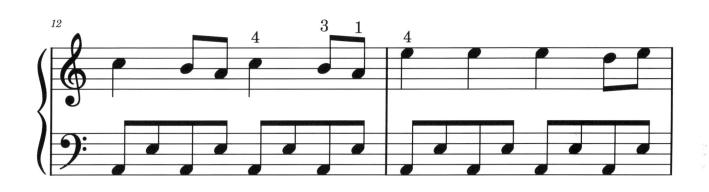

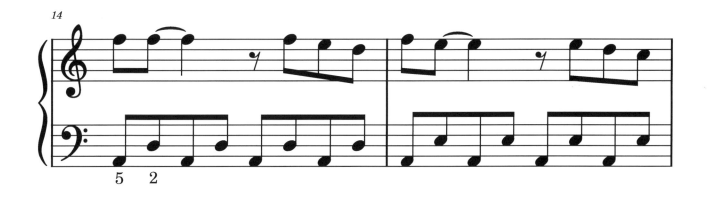

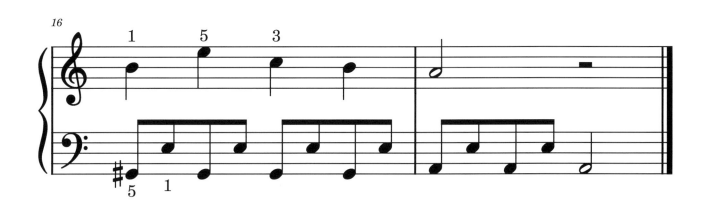

Die Gedanken Sind Frei

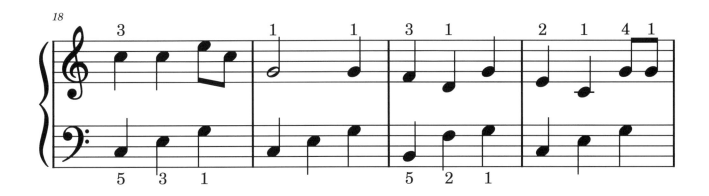

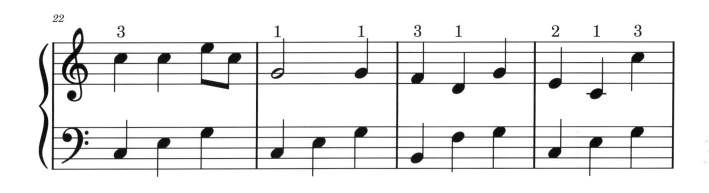

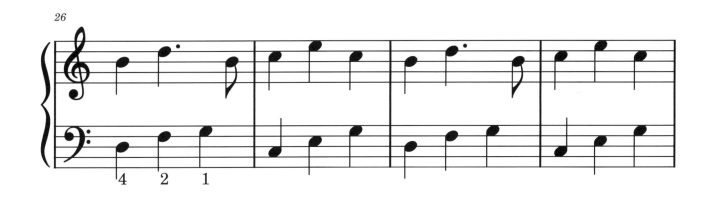

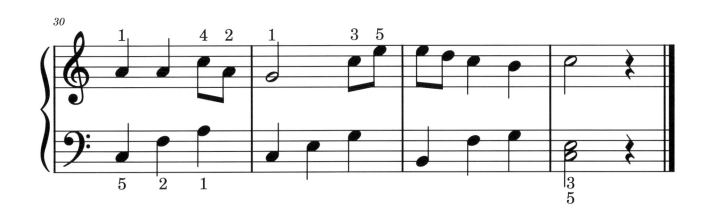

Greensleeves

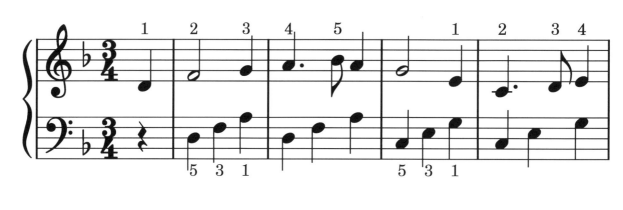

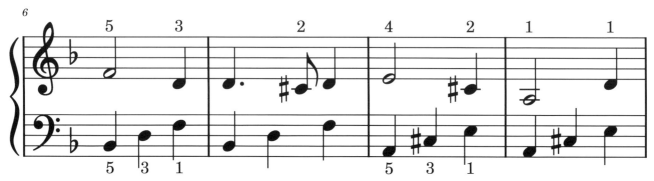

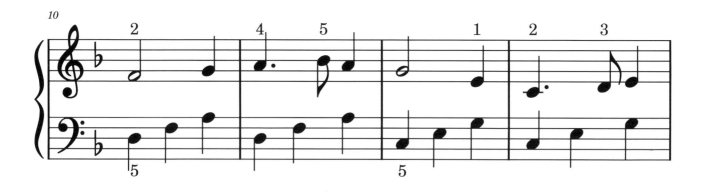

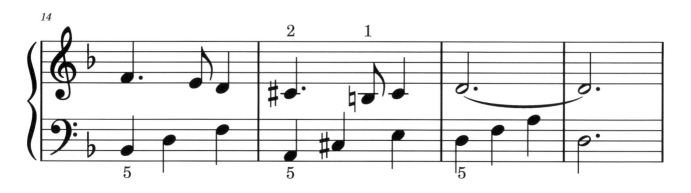

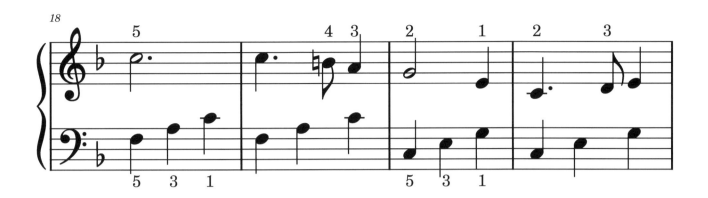

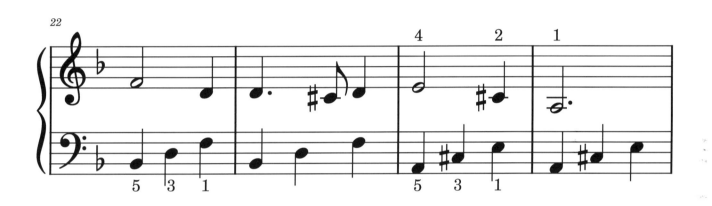

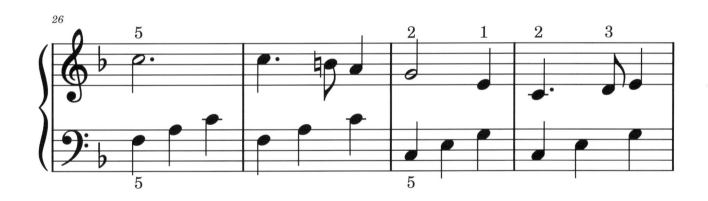

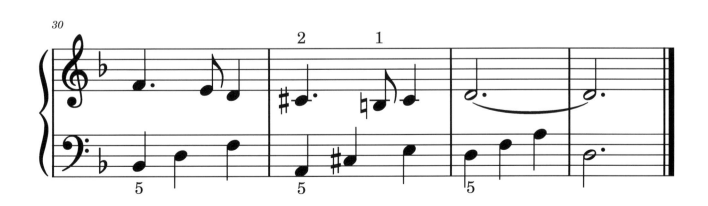

Red River Valley

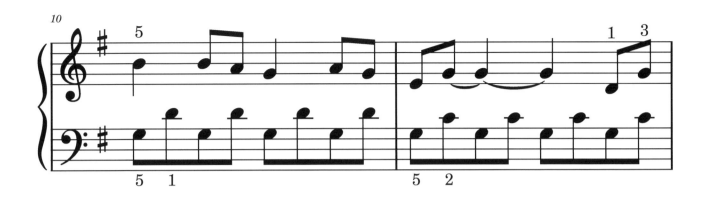

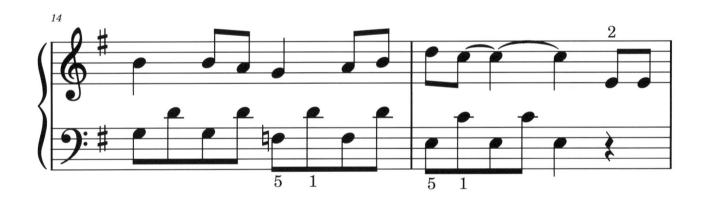

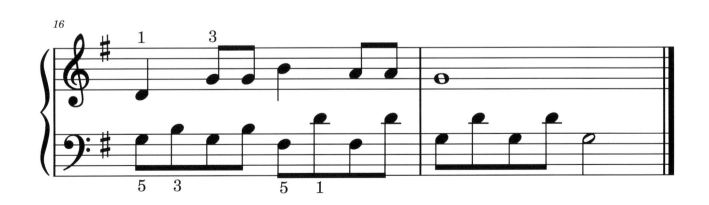

My Bonnie Lies Over The Ocean

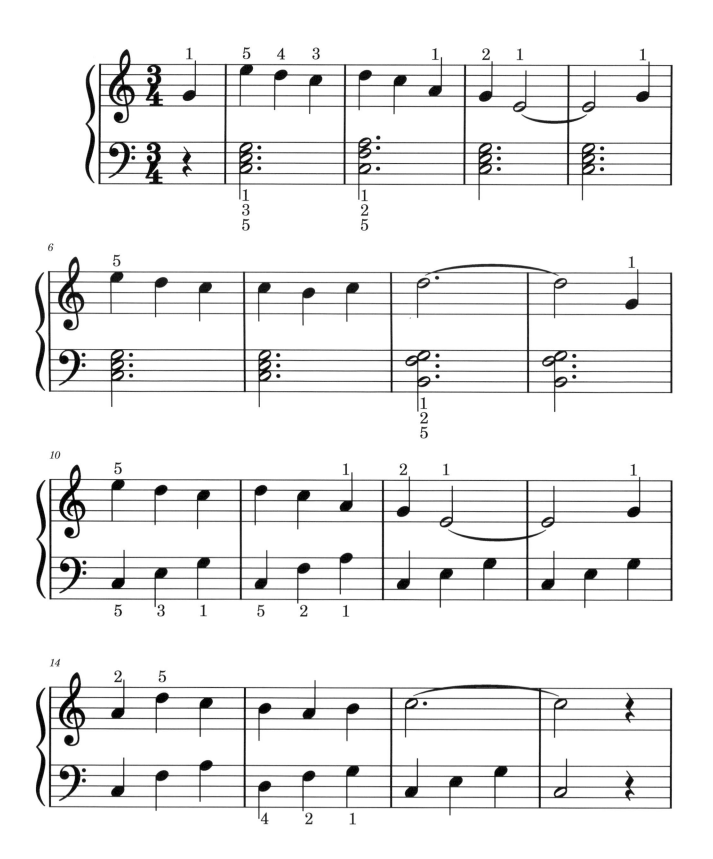

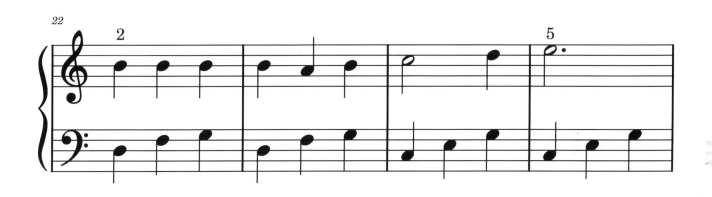

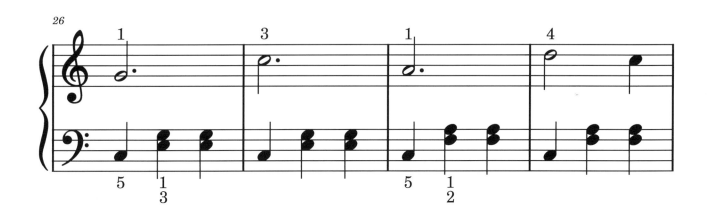

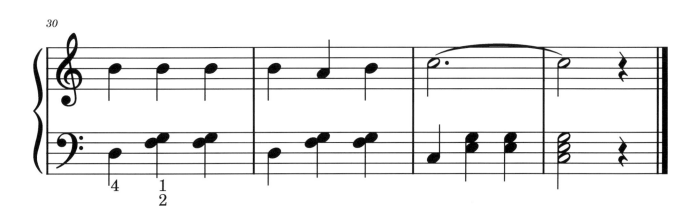

The Entertainer

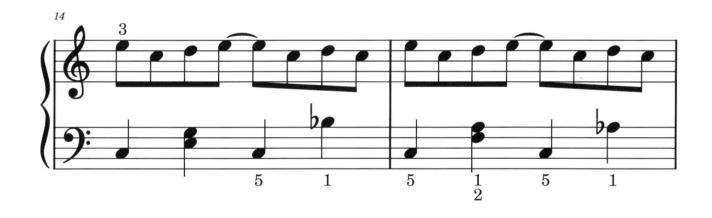

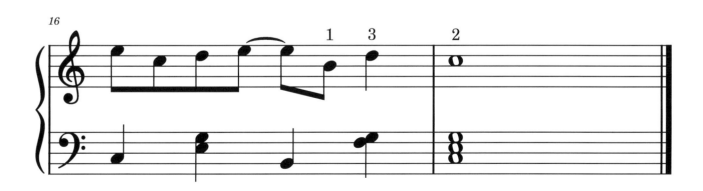

Printed in Great Britain
by Amazon

28982160R00055